Lilies of the Field

Lilies of the Field

Meditations for the Church Year

Translated and Edited by
Janice and Philip Wickeri

Wang Weifan

UPPER
ROOM BOOKS

Cover Painting by He Huibing
Cover design by C.J. Helms
First Upper Room Printing: August 1993 (3)
Second Upper Room Printing: March 1996 (2)
Library of congress Catalog Number 93-60486
ISBN 0-8358-0688-X

Printed in the United States of America

Preface

Wang Weifan's father died when he was seven years old, and his mother, a devout Buddhist, quailed at what life as a widow with a young son, dependent upon relatives, might be like. She nearly ended both their lives with opium poison. But as Rev. Wang says· when telling this story, for the sake of her son, she chose to live a life of hardship and humiliation. This left the boy with a deep sense that his life was a gift and should be lived for others.

Rev. Wang's personal history might serve as a biography of the Chinese church in dialogue with Chinese culture and society. His mother's habit of meditation and willingness to sacrifice herself for her children had a formative influence on his own character. He writes of her example: "this mother love with its reflection of Christ which led me three years after her death to a Christ who seemed already familiar and which further led me to dedicate myself in repaying the Lord's grace as a pastoral worker."

Through her reading of Buddhist scripture, his mother also passed on to him an abiding love for the Chinese literary tradition. He studied Chinese literature at Central University in Nanjing and his lectures at Nanjing Union Theological Seminary where he is now Associate Professor of New Testament often begin with the explication of a Chinese poem written on the classroom chalkboard. This is one of the ways in which he nurtures a new generation of Chinese Christian writers. The reader will find a number of references to the Chinese literary and cultural tradition in *Lilies of the Field* as well. In the original Chinese version, a number of the selections were written in the cadences of classical Chinese, and a contemporary translation was included in the Shanghai edition to assist the modern reader.

A native of Taizhou in northern Jiangsu, Wang Weifan became a Christian in 1947 while at the university in Nanjing, where he was active in the Intervarsity Christian Fellowship and the local church. He attributes his conversion to Miss Margurite Mazell, one hundred years old in 1993, whom he revisited forty-five years later during his first trip to the USA.

Rev. Wang attended Zhonghua Seminary in the beautiful lakeside city of Hangzhou and then moved to Nanjing when Nanjing Union Theological Seminary was formed in 1952, graduating from that institution three years later.

Like many Christian intellectuals of his generation, Wang Weifan was criticized during the anti-rightist campaign of 1958 and again during the Cultural Revolution and spent the better part of the next twenty years away from his theological work, separated from home and family as a result. Yet, contrary to what might be expected, he does not dwell on his own difficulties during these years but emphasizes the unexpected benefit these experiences brought: Chinese Christians returned to their own people; and the church, though not made perfect, was tempered through suffering. In the spirit of Isaiah 53 he emphasizes the love that transcends suffering and makes us whole again, speaking of "the tiny church of China, which was identified with its people in suffering, and in suffering has built itself up." He expresses a strong sense of hope for the future, one which is shaped by a theological perspective on history and nature in the embrace of the cosmic Christ. There can be no artificial distinctions drawn between individual and community, body and soul, history and eternity in this way of thinking.

For Wang Weifan, the mystical and the socio-political are not mutually exclusive but rather interacting or even complementary modes of discourse. Here is an evangelical thinker for whom change provides new opportunities for witness bearing, and a socially committed intellectual who is not afraid to say that he is sustained by the gracious love of God in Jesus Christ. Throughout

Wang Weifan's *Lilies of the Field*, one has the sense of being drawn into a spiritual journey that represents a path of renewal and hope. Christocentric mysticism is the thread running through Wang Weifan's life and thought, linking the habit of meditation he learned from his Buddhist mother and his evangelical spiritual life. His thought is informed by the encounter of Christian faith with traditional Chinese values recast in the twists and turns experienced by the Chinese people over the last forty-five years. This perspective brings him into conversation with people in the larger Christian community, in the same way that those of a Thomas Merton or a Julian of Norwich do. Although *Lilies of the Field* was written in China for Chinese Christians, its insights into our own spiritual lives transcend culture and history. In his own words, "Perhaps we can see culture as a mirror; different cultures being different mirrors. But in each mirror alike we find some aspect of Christ is reflected."

In addition to teaching New Testament, Wang Weifan serves as head of the Publications Department at Nanjing Union Theological Seminary. He is a moving preacher and well-known as the author of numerous biblical and historical studies and theological essays; as well as devotions, prayers, and hymns. Selections from *Lilies of the Field* began to appear in *Tian Feng*, the Chinese Christian monthly, in the early 1980s. In 1985, these were collected and published in Shanghai as a book of devotions and quickly sold out in churches. Chinese Christians found in *Lilies of the Field* a precious source of spiritual nourishment that could serve as a daily companion for prayer, reflection, and Bible study. The book has also been well received by educated young people and non-Christian intellectuals, for whom it has been a spiritually compelling introduction to the biblical message and the Christian way, written by a Chinese intellectual firmly rooted in his own social and cultural tradition.

The selections that appear in this edition of *Lilies of the Field* represent slightly more than half the number in the Chinese edition, but include several that Wang Weifan has written since its publication, some especially for seasons of the Christian year. The selections have been arranged to begin with the first Sunday in Advent so that the book may be used for Sunday readings and reflection.

I would like to thank Philip Wickeri for his excellent contribution to this book as cotranslator and editor. Both of us would like to express our gratitude to Rev. Wang Weifan for generously sharing his time, his work, and his enthusiasm with us. Weifan, this book is for you.

Janice K. Wickeri
Hong Kong

Lilies of the Field

By way of preface . . .
Consider the lilies of the field (Matthew 6:28)

The beauty of life does not lie in what we put on, but in bearing life's hardships without losing sight of its charm, in encountering the vagaries of the world without losing sight of its beauty. The adornments that the Father gives to his daughters and sons are carved and painted in the deepest recesses of the soul.

The tiny flowers of the field ask nothing for themselves and covet nothing. They are silent; but in their silence, they adorn the field. Their lives are brief; they appear quickly, go quickly. Yet their conscience is clear, and they leave behind their fragrance to the land that nourished them.

Wang Weifan

Meditations for

Advent

降臨期

But emptied himself (Philippians 2:7)

C hrist, Son of God, preceded all creation. He is in the image of God, with all of God's majesty, power, and glory. Yet he was willing to be humbled, even to be a servant.

It was precisely because he was humbled to the lowest that God exalted him to the highest, above all things. Though he was rich, he became poor for our sake. And because he was poor, God made him the heir of all creation.

He cared for neither power nor position, nor did he seek them. He willingly humbled himself, and therefore God filled him with all things. He poured himself out, but God filled him, that all things might find their richness in him.

When will I learn, O God, to see poverty as riches, to see humility as exaltation, to find plenty in emptiness, and empty myself, so that I may be filled with all of creation?

But to fulfill them *(Matthew 5:17)*

Christ was preexistent before history began and is above and outside of history. But he was willing to enter history, so that history could be united with all of eternity.

Christ did not destroy history. He came to fulfill it, that all which is good in history might be affirmed, made whole, raised up, and made holy.

The Christ who entered history was more than a descendant of David. Jesus Christ was the Son of Humanity, for he belongs to all people. Christ came to fulfill not only the history of the people of Israel, but the history of all peoples.

All peoples must seek Christ in the midst of the struggles of their own nations. Each nation in itself is incomplete. Yet it is in this incompleteness that the people of a nation await the acceptance, the blessing, and the fulfillment that is Christ. History cannot complete itself, nor do the people in history have the power to save themselves. It is Christ's saving grace that enables human history and people in history to see their everlasting home one day.

Keeping watch and the Comforter *(Luke 2:25, AP)*

The words of the poem ring true:

> *Cut off from our forebears and descendants,*
> *thinking of our long drawn-out days on this*
> *earth, alone and in sorrow,*
> *I burst into tears.*

This is the solitary life of the one who keeps watch, the historical loneliness of the watchman. Before the Comforter of a people arrives, those who keep watch can find no comfort or consolation. Consolation will be theirs only after their people are comforted.

The histories of the peoples of this world are histories of calamity, hardship, sadness, and bitterness. Caught up in the ebb and flow of historical change, all peoples look for the coming of Christ. Christ is not the glory of the people of Israel alone. Christ is also the great light of the gentiles. He is the Comforter of the house of Jacob and of all nations.

When, O Lord, when will you wipe away our mortal tears? When will all sorrow, crying, and pain be consigned to the past for all eternity?

His name shall be called Emmanuel (Matthew 1:23)

"Its outspread wings will fill the breadth of your land, O Emmanuel." This was the cry of the prophet Isaiah; this was what he had seen in a vision.

Where the waters of the river overflow its banks, I entreat you, Emmanuel, spread your wings and protect your children from the flood! Where famine yet rages, I entreat you, O Emmanuel, spread your wings, protect your children from starvation! Where the butcher's knife sheds the blood of innocents, I entreat you, O Emmanuel, spread your wings, protect your children that their corpses shall not cover the wilderness!

O Emmanuel, you provide for the birds of the air. How can you allow humanity, created in your image, to die on the barren earth? Abel's blood cried out to you from the earth, and you sought after him. Can you then allow the blood of innocents to be shed?

O Emmanuel, spread your wings, I entreat you. Fill the breadth of your land and cover your children who dwell here.

Meditations for

Christmas

聖誕節

He came to his own home (John 1:11)

Bright moon, scattered stars, so solitary is creation. The universe that God has created is especially silent on this night. It waits with bated breath for the Lord of Creation to return. The universe belongs to God; it is God's home.

Silence reigns supreme. The flowers of the field sway gently in the moonlight. This night, the vast earth awaits the homecoming of our Creator God. The vast earth and open fields belong to God; they are God's home.

Bethlehem lies dreaming. In his gentle mother's arms the babe sleeps peacefully this night. The City of David awaits the homecoming of David's descendant. The town of Bethlehem belongs to him; it is his home.

My bones, my flesh, my blood, my lungs, and my heart, were all made by God's hand. This night, my heart is at peace, awaiting my Creator's return. My heart belongs to God; it is God's home.

You will find a babe *(Luke 2:12)*

In the dimness of the stable, faint candlelight glimmers. Under the lamplight, a newborn babe lies in the manger. Serene, he utters no cry. Christ has chosen to enter the world, which itself was created through him.

The first small smile creases his little face. How like the first Adam. But this small smile also holds a love and obedience that will meet suffering on the road to the cross.

This small breast, gently rising and falling, is yet boundless beyond compare. How else could Christ embrace his innumerable prodigal children who are scattered far and wide? These tiny shoulders, delicate as jade, are yet strong as metal or stone. How else could they bear the burden of our human suffering and concern?

Sleep well, holy infant, may you be wrapped in swaddling clothes of deep love. Sleep well, holy infant, there is a manger in my heart for you.

For mine eyes have seen thy salvation (Luke 2:30)

Simeon's heart was weighed down by the oppression of his people. Who can tell what long years this old man had waited for the coming of God's salvation? Though Jesus was still an infant in his parents' arms when he came to the temple, Simeon experienced a sense of release in his heart and a sense of peace. At long last, before he was called to rest, he had seen God's salvation in Jesus Christ.

All God's servants should have hearts like this. If we have felt the distress and oppression of God's people, then we should be able to experience a sense of release and inner peace when saving grace and consolation come. But have we ever felt distress on behalf of the church, and not just for ourselves? Have we waited for salvation, not just for ourselves, but for the church? And when Jesus came to his temple, were our eyes open wide? Were our hands stretched forth in anticipation?

O God, grant that your spirit may move us to enter your temple. Open our eyes that we may see your saving grace, and stretch forth our hands to receive the Lord who has come.

Meditations for
Epiphany
顯現節

From the East *(Matthew 2:1)*

C hrist, the savior of humankind, is the great light that shines upon all peoples. But the very first to be called to worship the holy infant were the wise men from the East. Why them, in particular? Was it that the ancient cultures of the East had received more of God's revelation and were thus better prepared to accept Christ? Or was it that the East stood in greater need of Christ because of the endless river of tears that is its history? I do not know. Perhaps the answer lies in the star that lighted their path.

What I do know is that the East, in its recent history, has been hammered on the anvil of extreme adversity, forged and tempered for over a hundred years. Precisely because of this, should not the East be able to offer up an even more refined gold when it worships Christ? Out of this pain and agony, should not the East be ready to bring forth even more fragrant frankincense and myrrh?

The wise men have already returned home, because people from the East have a deep sense of attachment to their native places. And yet, they haven't really gone far from the manger. Don't you see them still, kneeling over the infant?

And a sword will pierce through your own soul also

(Luke 2:35)

As the holy infant Jesus was being dedicated to God in the temple, Simeon prophesied to Mary: "And a sword will pierce through your own soul also."

When Jesus called out from the cross, "My God, my God, why have you forsaken me?" The heavenly Father hid his countenance from Jesus because he bore the sins of humanity. On earth his mother, whom "all generations would call . . . blessed," fell to the ground at the foot of the cross, weeping. The pain of losing her son was like a sharp and merciless sword piercing Mary's soul.

Yet the true meaning of "blessed" is contained in this: to be of one heart with God; to know God's greatness; to be willing to give one's only son on the sacrificial altar for the sake of God's eternal plan!

O Father, you gave your only begotten son for the salvation of humankind. All we have, we have from you. Forgive our selfishness. May we return all we have to you, from whence it came, that your will be done.

Become like children (Matthew 18:3)

A child's heart is clear as crystal, so unlike my own, which is full of flaws. The longer I am on this earth, the more sullied I become, the more clouded my eyesight. Yet it is impossible to bring my heart back to that pristine state of childhood when it was a piece of white jade.

A child's heart responds to others sincerely. My heart is twisted and heavy with selfishness. A child's heart is humble while mine is proud, modest where mine is haughty.

A child's heart is yielding as water, while mine is unbending as iron or stone. Because of this, the eyes of my heart barely see the tiny light of the soul; the ears of my heart can barely hear its tiny voice.

Help me, O God. Turn me around; give me a child-like heart; let me become like a child once again. I want to be like my lord Jesus Christ, gentle and humble. I want to follow his example, ever bearing his yoke on my own shoulders.

That they may be one (John 17:22)

Before he left this earth, Jesus prayed that the disciples might be one. Likewise, the Holy Spirit has bestowed unity on the church of Christ.

Knowledge and insight cannot make the church one. Pride and a sense of self-importance are obstacles to Christian unity. Only a loving heart that comes from holy love can unite the church.

Unity is not conformity but rather a kind of harmony. It has its source in the yielding and generosity of a loving heart. Unity does not mean annexation or being swallowed up. Rather, it implies a life together that finds its source in the understanding and gentleness of a loving heart.

A church that is moving toward unity glorifies Christ and comforts the Holy Spirit. We need only put forth a loving heart to heal the wounds of yesterday. We cannot allow old wounds to break open and bleed again through our own narrowness and bias.

How is it that you sought me?
(Luke 2:49)

Jn the course of our spiritual journey, it often happens that we think Jesus is still at our side when actually he hasn't been walking with us for some time. And far more than once, when we have gone seeking him with hurt feelings, his response has been, "How is it that you have sought me?" But we have never understood his words, because we do not understand his heart.

We are also going to Jerusalem, but we only go at the appointed times, following the rules. We make our sacrifice, we keep our "Passover," but when we have done what is required, we return to our own path, assuming that Christ will be with us on the way we have laid out for ourselves. The result is that day by day, year after year, we walk without God.

O Lord, help us to understand what is in your heart, to follow in your footsteps. Save us from our own stupidity, in which we expect you to follow us. Amen.

You have been faithful over a little *(Matthew 25:21)*

People have different gifts. What Christ requires of us and the tasks that are entrusted to us differ accordingly.

God surely will not require of us what is greater than our strength. God simply requires loyalty in a few things. We are called to pour ourselves out according to what has been given to us.

The rewards of work are neither honor nor prizes; even less money or position. The rewards of work are yet more work and a share in the joy of Jesus Christ.

Let us hearken to Christ's voice: "Well done, good and faithful servant; you have been faithful over a little, I will set you over much; enter into the joy of your master!"

Meditations for
Lent
受難期

For this purpose I have come to this hour (John 12:27)

The bitter cup of humankind's redemption through his death on the cross was before him. Jesus asked: "Take this cup from me." But he also said, "Not my will, but thine be done."

In the moment when he faced the extreme suffering of being forsaken by God due to the sins of the world, Jesus begged: "If it is possible, let this pass." But he also said, "For this purpose I have come to this hour."

How precious are the struggles we encounter in this life. There inevitably comes a time when we too must pay some price for others, even the ultimate price.

When that time comes, will our prayer be, "Let this moment pass?" Or will it be, "For this purpose I have come to this hour?"

O Jesus, Lamb of God, save us from the struggles and bitterness of Gethsemane. But also enable us to follow you to the foot of the cross on Golgatha! Amen.

J know how to be abased, and J know how to abound *(Philippians 4:12)*

Paul knew how to endure poverty; in the midst of want, he "coveted no one's silver or gold or apparel," preferring to toil with his own hands to meet his own needs and the needs of those who were with him.

He knew how to respond to plenty; he accepted the Philippians' gifts as he would the most beautiful and fragrant offering, "a sacrifice acceptable and pleasing to God," and did not dare to waste them or ask for more.

"Riches cannot corrupt nor want cause him to abandon his integrity." Such was the high standard the ancients set themselves. Uncorrupted by wealth, retaining integrity in poverty: should not this also be the conduct of sons and daughters of God as they tread the spiritual path?

A thorn *(2 Corinthians 12:7)*

I go forward; I halt, all at God's command. The key is in God's hand, the door God's to open or close. When I achieve something in my work, the glory belongs to God, but I am selfish and secretly reserve it for myself. God's door stands open, as usual, when I return all glory to God. If it shuts for a moment, it is to avoid my pride and boastfulness.

Everyone has a thorn in the flesh, a trouble that cannot be overcome or some personal failing. The spirit is willing, but the flesh is weak. God does not remove the thorn but promises grace. The omnipotence and power of God cover me. When I am weak, God's power shines forth more clearly. My strength is but weakness. Except for God's grace, what can I rely on? Of what shall I boast?

I am but a vessel of clay. There is no fountainhead of grace save the Lord. Let me be even more humble lest I obstruct the Lord's work. My part is to pour myself out. All glory belongs to God. How dare I take it for myself!

Then again he laid his hands upon his eyes *(Mark 8:22-25)*

After Christ had laid his hands upon the blind man of Bethsaida, he was able to see people, but they looked like trees walking. Not until Christ had again laid hands upon his eyes was he cured and able to see everything clearly.

People certainly do not look like trees. You would have to stand them on their heads to achieve even a slight resemblance. So the people the blind man first saw were topsy-turvy. The world he saw was an upside-down world. Not until Christ had laid his hands upon his eyes a second time did the man see people who looked like people, a world returned to its right aspect.

As children of God, we need Jesus to lay his hands upon us a second time, because we never see things clearly. We always tend to see upside-down images. O God have mercy upon us. Lay your hands upon our eyes once again, that we may see clearly the world that you made for what it is. Amen.

He . . . rebuked them (Luke 9:51-56)

When they saw that Jesus was on his way to Jerusalem, the Samaritan villagers would not receive him. James and John wanted Jesus to call down fire from heaven upon this village to consume those who would not receive him. But Jesus rebuked them saying, "You do not know what manner of spirit you are of; for the Son of man came not to destroy human lives but to save them."

The disciples' hearts were those of destroyers, not of saviors. Yet in Jesus, we discover the heart of one who saves. The disciples would curse, as the prophet Jonah did, and then wait for Nineveh to be consumed. Theirs were not the loving hearts of the God who loves the people and even the animals of this created world.

Christ preferred to move on to another village, and so he left the village of the Samaritans without even a word of reproach, let alone a curse. He left quietly, and we can imagine that in this silence there was much forgiveness, patience, and deep emotion born of his eternal love. This was Christ's response. How then shall we act in similar situations?

[The King] who comes in the name of the Lord (John 12:13)

P alm branches in hand, shouting "Hosanna!" the people of Jerusalem surge out of the city to meet the king who comes in the name of the Lord. But this king does not arrive in a war chariot nor on a prancing stallion. He is mounted on a lowly ass. He is mighty, but humble too; he is glorious and yet ordinary. He is a king without a kingdom, a lord without the airs of a lord.

He is Lord, but he serves his disciples as a servant. He is king, but he had not ascended a throne in a palace. His throne awaits him at Golgotha, and his kingly title hangs on the cross. This is the meaning of the Lord of lords, the King of kings, whose name every tongue shall praise and before whom every knee shall bow. Christ's majesty and glory are contained within humility and shame. He has given himself up and has borne abandonment by God. Yet in his weakness, he attracts and wins over humankind!

Meditations for
Holy Week
受難週

He was hungry *(Matthew 21:18)*

Jesus Christ, the incarnate son of humankind, experienced physical hunger and thirst. But his spiritual hunger and thirst were even greater.

Adam's departure from Eden marked the beginning of humankind's feelings of spiritual loss. Throughout the ages, people have continued to search for peace in an eternal dwelling place. But no one has ever been able to find peace unless he or she has first found God.

Adam's departure from Eden also marked the beginning of the Creator's search for humankind. The elderly father in the parable of the prodigal son must have been waiting anxiously at the gate for his child's return. Similarly, God can find no peace until all prodigal sons and daughters return from their wandering.

Christ came into the world with this hunger and thirst for God within himself. God in Christ left Eden in order to seek and to save us long lost mortals.

When my heart rests in God, then too will God gain peace through me. Only then will Christ's hunger and thirst be satisfied.

The very stone which the builders rejected (Mark 12:10)

There is a lofty temple in heaven, and Christ is its cornerstone. Throughout the Bible, we see that whenever those who are chosen to be the builders of the heavenly kingdom reject God, their efforts come to nothing.

The church is also a heavenly temple whose cornerstone is Christ. If we, as workers for the Lord, do not build upon this cornerstone, then all our efforts will come to naught. There is also a heavenly kingdom in our hearts, and there too Christ must be the cornerstone. If we would reject this cornerstone, our spiritual development will also count as nothing.

Christ is our one foundation and only cornerstone. Outside of Christ, there is no support. Outside of Christ, we have nothing to rely upon.

But you will not always have me
(Mark 14:7)

T here was a home that Jesus loved in Bethany, a home that had given him much comfort and warmth. This is the last day and the last night that the Lord spent there; and after today, he would never return.

This day in Bethany, there was a farewell dinner at which not a word was said, for language is utterly incapable of giving expression to the love we have for our Lord Jesus Christ. The woman who poured the ointment, therefore, did so without a sound. She was pouring out all her love for Jesus Christ, as a farewell.

The ointment worth 300 denarii was certainly very dear. But how can we attach a price in silver or in gold to a heart that loves our Lord Jesus Christ? How can love be measured in those terms? It is true that concern for the poor is a good deed that is pleasing to God. But what good deed can ever replace the loving heart that God requires of each of us?

Peter followed at a distance
(Luke 22:54)

After supper, Jesus went to the Mount of Olives in the Garden of Gethsemane. His heart was deeply troubled. Though I followed Jesus into the garden, I was not able to keep watch with him but fell deeply asleep, leaving him alone with his worries. I am Peter.

When he was taken to the high priest's house, I only followed at a distance, because I was afraid. When he was mocked and insulted, I denied him three times and allowed him to be beaten black and blue.

Before Pilate, Jesus was condemned to death. How heavy that cross must have been. How was my Lord to carry it? Simon of Cyrene carried it behind Jesus. But I watched from the sidelines, letting him stumble along as he went.

Jesus has now gone far away, to a hill outside the city where he will suffer and die. It is for me that he suffers, for me that he dies. But I could not follow him to the cross, and so I let him drink the cup of bitterness alone.

When I think of these things, my heart is deeply troubled. Though I would give my body to be broken, how can I return the love of Christ?

There they crucified him (John 19:18)

Who is this man, head crowned with thorns? It is my Lord, King of kings, Christ Jesus. Why does he carry the cross towards Golgotha? He is the sacrificial lamb, led silently to the slaughter. Why is this man nailed to a cross on Golgotha? He is without sin, yet he dies for us sinners. He bears the sins of humankind and is offered up on the sacrificial altar.

Why do water and blood flow from this man's side?

If blood did not flow, how would my sins be washed away? His blood is the fount of my salvation. And so I kneel at the foot of the cross. The cross is the beginning of my life and the source to which it returns. The cross is now my life's sign and its altar.

Meditations for
Easter
復活節

They laid Jesus there (John 19:42)

He was laid in an empty tomb. Just so is a grain of wheat planted in the ground. The darkness, the cold, the solitude, the bitterness of death all turned him in the direction of eternal life and a new day.

If I search carefully in the dark places, I will be able to get a glimpse of the brilliance that penetrates the whole universe. If I bend my ear to the silent places, I will be able to hear the thunder that shakes this vast land. Christ, the Son of God, was willing to be humbled to the lowest point. He will therefore be raised on high and receive the praises of all on heaven and on earth.

If Christ had not been humbled, how could he be lifted up? If there were no death, how could there be new life? Without darkness, how could there be light? Without stillness, how could we hear sounds?

"Without winter, how could we greet the arrival of spring?" These are the laws of nature. Are the laws of the spirit any different?

He is not here *(Matthew 28:6)*

The stone had been rolled away, and our Lord Jesus Christ had risen from the dead. He was no longer in the tomb. Neither the tomb nor death could hold him.

The long night is over. The first rays of the morning sun shine across the land. Christ is not in the long night. How could the night hold back the dawn, its morning light breaking through the rosy clouds?

The opaque shadows have been dispersed, the light of the sun plays upon the tomb. Christ is not in the shadows, for shadows and chill cannot swallow warmth and light!

Of what importance are the sighs and weaknesses of yesterday? Christ does not dwell in weakness or defeat. He is the Lord, now strong and victorious, who rose from the dead.

Why wallow in suffering and despair? Christ dwells not in these things, for he is the Lord, confident and hopeful, who rose from the dead!

Why are we rendered helpless by difficulties? Christ does not dwell in our difficulties and inaction, for he is the Lord of life, the Creator who has risen from the dead!

That . . . no one will deprive me of my ground for boasting *(1 Corinthians 9:15, NRSV)*

Those who preach the gospel must depend on it for their livelihood. This was God's original command. But Paul never made use of this right to support himself in dealing with the church in Corinth. He often accepted things from the church in Philippi, but from the Corinthians he took nothing, so that those hostile to him would have no grounds for complaint.

"For I would rather die, than have anyone deprive me of my ground for boasting." Such was the spiritual integrity of Paul. All God's daughters and sons, all God's workers, should have spiritual integrity like this.

The Chinese church's grounds for boasting are precisely that she asks nothing in return for doing God's work, but says with Paul, "I would rather die, than have anyone deprive me of my ground for boasting."

Always carrying in the body the death of Jesus (2 Corinthians 4:10, NRSV)

The Chinese philosopher Mencius once said: "Misery and hardship are life-giving; a life of carefree ease leads unto death." If this is our experience in the life of the flesh, how much more in the life of the spirit!

Bland comfort cannot help us progress in life. We are tempered by setbacks and trained through difficulty.

Paul followed the Lord throughout his life, and Paul's was a life of misery and hardship. Yet, it was this very hardship, poverty, hunger, thirst, and cold suffered for the sake of Jesus Christ that became the "death of Jesus," which Paul always carried with him and through which "the life of Jesus" was manifest in Paul.

Human life never runs smoothly; we meet with terrifying waves and stormy seas. But the spirit grows most amidst stormy seas and tempering blasts!

Lord, grant that in your death, we may find your life.

So [life] is at work in us *(2 Corinthians 4:12)*

If not for the sweat of the gardener, flowers would have no beauty or fragrance. Children would not grow healthy and strong without the efforts of their parents. Without the sufferings and sacrifices of their forebears, succeeding generations would not know well-being and happiness.

This is one aspect of the truth of death and resurrection: even as the wheat will not sprout until the seed falls to the earth and dies, the church could not be established or grow to maturity without the toil and tears of the apostles. If death is not at work in us, life cannot be at work in others.

O God, lead us into the truth of death and resurrection that we may live for others, giving willingly of our sweat and toil, begrudging not even exhaustion and death.

Forgetting what lies behind and straining forward to what lies ahead
(Philippians 3:13)

It is difficult to forget the past. But as we go on our spiritual journey, intoxication with past achievements can make us complacent and rigid. If we wallow in past disappointments, we will hesitate to go forward. If we brood over past frustrations, it will be difficult to extricate ourselves from them. The past is water under the bridge. It is better to fix our eyes on what will be than to turn back to what was.

The road you must travel is far. This was God's call to Elijah as he rested under the broom tree. The road we must travel is equally long. When the glory of spring is spread before us, can we really want to be a withered tree? As a thousand sails sweep by, can we be content to be a sunken ship?

Lord, awaken our souls. Save us from exhaustion and confusion, that we no longer rest beneath our own broom tree, but, relying on the strength we have from God, continue to run the course that is set before us.

Our inner nature is being renewed every day (2 Corinthians 4:16)

Time and difficulties age the outer nature, but they do not necessarily afflict the inner nature with despondency and exhaustion. Even physical impairment need not be a matter for regret. Haven't we all come across many heroes in this world "broken in body but whole in spirit"?

All God's daughters and sons, all God's workers, should have spiritual integrity like this. The Chinese philosopher Chuang Tzu observed: "There is nothing worse than the death of the heart." This is the greatest tragedy because it suggests that a person's spiritual life is teetering on the brink of hopelessness. A heart inexhaustible, an "inner nature" that is being renewed every day and that neither ice nor snow can harm nor storms overcome; in the eyes of God, these are most precious.

God, give me inner strength to help me become a tent-post in this earthly tent. I rely on you, that what is mortal be swallowed up by eternal life. In this world, let me live for you.

Meditations for

Ascension

耶穌昇天日

Why do you stand looking into heaven? (Acts 1:11)

W hy do you stand looking into heaven?

Though Jesus Christ has ascended to heaven and sits at the right hand of God, he is still in our hearts, yours and mine. Christ surrounds us. He listens and is watching. The hands of Jesus Christ still soothe our wounds, yours and mine.

A rising sun, Christ ascends to heaven, emitting light that covers the mountains and fills the valleys. Jesus Christ is our North Star, brilliant and crystal clear, glimmering in the far reaches of the cosmos, guiding us home, you and me.

Christ, who has transcended time and space, still remains within creation and history. Christ upholds creation and guides human history. All that came from God is in the end guided back to God through Christ.

Our life is already in Christ and yet remains hidden within God. It unfolds in heaven and on earth as a drama played for the angels and the world to see.

Has the potter no right over the clay? (Romans 9:21)

God is the potter; we are the clay. As the potter molds the vessel so are we shaped by the potter's hands.

We may have been rejected as useless by the world, but God's profound grace will never abandon us. God will turn the potter's wheel and form us anew. God has the power to shape us as God sees fit.

God has the power to mold us into vessels for beauty and the power to make us into vessels for menial use. Whatever God does, I am content as long as I can be made useful. But Lord, do not let me defy you, becoming a vessel for wrath awaiting destruction. The vessel may be small, but it seeks the riches of your mercy.

Though I be shattered, I will not complain; for God will gather up the pieces, and when they have been ground to dust and mixed back into the clay, God will work them anew and shape me for use, in order to realize God's beautiful plan.

God is my Lord. Can I compare the potter to the clay? Resist God's will? I am but God's creation and God my Creator!

Meditations for

Pentecost

聖靈降臨節

Speaking foreign languages (Acts 2:6, AP)

After Babel, you and I were separated by vast distances, at opposite ends of the earth, never to meet again.

After Babel, our languages were muddled. People had no way of sharing their innermost feelings. They were filled with misunderstanding and suspicion.

But at Pentecost, tongues of fire came down from heaven, and the disciples were able to speak in the language of each one in the multitude. Thus they bore witness to Christ. Our common language was differentiated through human sin. By the grace of the Holy Spirit, our many languages can become the means for sharing what we have in common.

For more than a hundred years, we in China tried to witness to our own people. But our sin made us appear before our sisters and brothers as outsiders. It was not only a common language that we had lost, but more. We had lost the soul nourished by the soil of our native place.

O Holy Spirit, bring us back to this heart we have lost and give us tongues of fire. How else can we bear witness to Christ in the presence of our people? Amen.

Chosen — Sprinkled with the blood of Christ — Sanctified (1 Peter 1:2, AP)

When God created the cosmos and all that is in it, the Holy Spirit, in the path of life eternal, also participated in the economy of creation. The source of all life can be traced to the movement of the Holy Spirit, spawning and begetting all that exists. The creation of humanity follows the same movement. The difference is that humanity was created in the image of God.

Humankind's fall does not alter God's choice and intention at the time of creation. The work of redemption is in this sense a continuation of the work of creation. We may renounce our faith in God, but God will never abandon us. Out of eternal love for humankind, God has bound himself to an everlasting covenant that will never be broken.

God chose to give up his beloved son Jesus Christ, that through the sprinkling of his blood, the sullied and twisted consciences of humankind might be cleansed. With her sighs, the Holy Spirit intercedes and moves people in the deepest recesses of the spirit, causing them to be sanctified, restoring them to human dignity and exalting them to the place of their Creator God.

Make straight the way of the Lord

(John 1:23, NRSV)

Why must we make straight the way of the Lord? Because there are so many twists and turns that when Christ comes into his own country, his own people do not receive him.

God looks with favor on the church. But so often Christ is forced to "leap upon the mountains and bound over the hills," or wait until "the day breathes and the shadows flee," or knock at the door asking, "Please let me come in." We are always putting up obstacles that prevent Christ from entering our lives.

Our ignorance carves out hollows in God's way. Our self-assurance throws up ridges, our vacillations create the twists and turns in the road. By our sense of self-importance and "holiness," we even shut God out.

Beloved God, may your wisdom fill our hollowness, and may your humility level the obstacles we put before you. May our way be made straight by the determination with which you walked to Golgotha. May your hands, wounded on the cross, yet stretched open to the whole world, open the door that lies ahead. Amen.

The genealogy of Jesus Christ
(Matthew 1:1)

It was not Matthew's intention simply to record the bloodline of Abraham and the house of David. Rather he wished to sum up the spiritual rise and fall of God's chosen people in Old Testament times.

With the apostles, the spiritual genealogy of Jesus Christ began to unfold. It had its ups and downs. Just as our own attitude toward God's revelation has been inconsistent, so the church in different times has wavered in its understanding of God's truth.

Jesus Christ's family line will never be cut off. But that family tree records both the descendants of Abraham and the stumbling blocks of our own history.

The church must reflect on its life in the light of the Holy Spirit. The daughters and sons of God must reflect on their individual lives too. We must ask, How will I appear on Christ's family tree when history turns a new page? What kind of addition will my name make?

J must decrease (John 3:30)

All who were baptized by John the Baptist followed Jesus. John's disciples may have felt this was unfair, but his reply was, "He must increase, but I must decrease." He said this because God had given him Elijah's ability of spirit. But this was only to prepare a suitable people for God, to prepare the way of the Lord.

The daughters and sons of God should store up much fruit, but they do not have the right to keep a single piece for themselves. They should lead others to Christ but must not lead others to follow themselves. The ministry of the spirit means that God must always increase, while we must decrease. Isn't this the way life should be? Shouldn't we decrease while others increase? On life's long journey, when we have received the baton from the one ahead and run our length of the race, then we must pass the baton on to one who runs faster than we. When that person has traveled over the road prepared by the one ahead, then he or she must be willing to pave the way for those who come after.

God, give me ability of spirit, that I may not fritter away this life. But grant me also humility and self-understanding to willingly decrease before God and others. Amen.

For we are his workmanship
(Ephesians 2:10)

We are his workmanship; as the craft to the crafter or the art to the artist, so are we to God.

Mountains and seas, the sky of night and the clouds of morning: these are God's vast canvas. Yet it gives him greater pleasure to leave the tiniest brush stroke on our hearts. God can sculpt myriad shapes among the eternity of seasons and the annals of history. Yet God finds greater happiness in leaving the mark of the carver's blade on each of us.

Throughout time, the saints have been as varied as the clouds, but each without exception is the product of God's hand. God toils and strives for perfection in me as if I am his sole creation.

Perhaps God pauses in the task now and again, to work out the design, to ponder the art. But more, God waits—for people are not mere strings on a harp. Once we have been lightly plucked, God is willing to wait for us to compose the loveliest of melodies ourselves.

But you are a chosen race, a royal priesthood, a holy nation, God's own people *(1 Peter 2:9)*

God has not chosen us to be God's people that we might live apart from others or place ourselves above them. Rather, God wants us to be a priesthood to represent the people at God's holy altar.

As priests, we must have shoulders that can support the multitude, arms capable of embracing them. We must be like the priests in the Old Testament, who wore shoulder clasps and breastplates mounted with precious stones and inscribed with the names of the twelve tribes of Israel.

We should be like our brothers and sisters in all things, not setting ourselves above them. If we act otherwise, we will not know the meaning of mercy and faithfulness. "Supermen" cannot represent the people, because Jesus came, not to save angels, but to save women and men, the descendants of Abraham.

As priests, we ourselves must be tested, otherwise it will be difficult for us to understand human weakness. And what is more, we must be conscious of our own weakness, otherwise we will have trouble understanding those lost in foolishness and confusion.

We have not been called because we are in any way superior to others. In fact, we are no different from anyone else, any more than the Levites were cleverer than the rest of the Israelites. Therefore, the honor of the priesthood is not something we can choose for ourselves. No one is worthy. God calls us to it.

You have kept the good wine until now *(John 2:10)*

Jesus' first miracle did not free anyone from the pain of serious illness or wipe away the distress of hunger or thirst. Instead, it was lighthearted, an occasion of happiness.

The miracle of the wedding feast at Cana says to us: there is joy on earth and God wants to enrich that joy, to make it full to overflowing. There is indeed good wine on earth to lift people's spirits, and the Lord tells his servant to bring the better wine when people have drunk their fill.

The saints have always comforted the afflicted and have cared for those in distress. But the Lord Jesus left the best wine until now; perhaps because he wanted us, in this generation, to join our joy to that of others; to be one song among the many.

Of the miracles recorded in John, two especially show forth the glory of God. One is the raising of Lazarus from the dead in the midst of his loved ones' tears; the other is here, where Jesus has kept the best wine till last for the revelers. Thus, the glory of God shines forth, not only in comfort to those who weep but also in the happiness of the joyous. For the song sung in chorus is always more beautiful than a solitary voice.

Buy from me . . . salve to anoint your eyes *(Revelation 3:18)*

The building up of the church and individual growth both require "gold refined by fire." Before gold has been refined it cannot be pure gold; it cannot turn spiritual poverty to wealth. But we also need a little salve, so that cloudy eyes may be brightened. Otherwise we cannot turn spiritual blindness to clarity.

The eyes of the flesh may be blind, but this does not keep one from seeing the light of truth. If the eyes of the spirit are clouded, however, the whole person will be plunged into darkness.

We cannot see clearly the light that illumines the entire way before us. Even with a lamp before our feet, we will need clear sight. Naturally the light is partial. It may cause us to "see, but . . . not understand." The value of the plea by the blind beggar Bartimaeus whom Jesus healed is that he asks for nothing but "that I may see."

Our eyes have been more blessed than those of the prophets of old or those of the righteous. They looked at what we do but did not see. We must hold fast to the promise God made to Nathaniel and ask that we may see yet greater things—even the heavens opening.

Be aglow with the Spirit *(Romans 12:11)*

If no fire of love blazes within you, your love for others may be false and insincere. Though you do all you can to help the poor, even giving your body to be burned, but do not have the holy love that comes from within, then it is possible that all you do stems only from a desire for compliments and fame.

Water, even a flood or the convergence of many streams, cannot extinguish the flame of love. Storms cannot dim it, neither snow nor frost kill it, nor threats shake it. Though death draws near, it will not be changed.

"Water does not freeze to a depth of three feet as the result of a single day's cold." To melt a long-frozen heart, one must intensify the warmth. Dying embers may not glow to life again. But it is difficult to catch fire alone—a spark must touch our souls. If we in ourselves are "cold as ice," how can we make others "bloom with color"?

The flames of love cannot be extinguished, nor the spark of love go out. Love, only this flame is eternal.

Love never ends *(1 Corinthians 13:8)*

The stream of love flows unending; like oceans it seethes unceasing.

My Lord is the source of love, I the river's course. Let God's love flow through me. I will not obstruct it.

Irrigation ditches can water but a portion of the field; the great Yangtze River can water a thousand acres. Expand my heart, O Lord, that I may love yet more people. The waters of love can cover vast tracts; nothing will be lost to me. The greater the outward flow, the greater the returning tide.

If I am not linked to love's source, I will dry up. If I dam the waters of love, they will stagnate.

Can I compare my heart with boundless seas? But abandon not the measure of my heart, O Lord. Let the waves of your love still billow there!

Everyone to whom much has been given, much will be required

(Luke 12:48, NRSV)

Nurtured and fed for days unto years, all that I am and all that I can do arise from the grace of God. All this is given, not for my own pleasure or adornment, but for service to God and others.

As vessels we differ from one another in size and in gifts. Yet if all alike have loyal and conscientious hearts, each one's ability will increase through use.

One who receives much must also do much. How can I always bury my gifts in the ground? And if I set them aside and do not make use of them, they will be taken from me and added to one who will use them willingly.

God has not entrusted me with these gifts so that I might use them to gain money or position, but that I might work more conscientiously, more diligently for my God. Because much has been given to me, I cannot remain at the pond's edge but must dare to venture forth, treading on thin ice!

My God is a stern God. From one to whom much is given, much will be required. From one to whom much is entrusted, much will be asked. If I have been unworthy of his profound mercy, how shall I fare when I stand before the judgment seat?

Jesus withdrew again to the mountain by himself *(John 6:15)*

O Lord, you healed one about to die of disease; you commanded the paralytic beside the pool to rise and walk. With a meager five loaves and two fish, you satisfied the five thousand. All this you did out of pity for the people to the glory of God the Father. Lord most great, you did not want to accept the people's adulation. When you had accomplished your task, you withdrew to the mountain alone.

Abject as I am, how dare I compare myself to you? For I am not like you. I can get involved but not withdraw. A little fame pleases me. Though the truth belies my reputation, fame intoxicates me. Withdrawal is unthinkable. Personal glory still counts for something with me. Vanity and selfishness, like polluted waters, still churn before my eyes.

A crystal sea spreads itself before God. In the sea, a fire blazes. May this holy fire ignite my heart, that I enter service to others in society as a red-hot flame. But may my inner self remain calm as that crystal sea, that when I withdraw into God's presence, I do so clear and untroubled by selfishness.

The weakness of God is stronger than human strength *(1 Corinthians 1:25, NRSV)*

The Father's omnipotence could not serve to save his Son. God loved Jesus Christ with a profound love, yet could not respond to his pleas. Hands vast as the heavens could not withhold the cup of bitterness. Eternal, mighty arms could not protect his only Son. The price of salvation was high, yet the Father had to pay it. Did he not love his Son? And yet, to save the multitude, the Son had to be forsaken.

Love's strength lies in letting go. God did not stint his Son. How much less then does he begrudge creation for us. Love's power is in its steadfastness. Neither life nor death can separate us from this love!

The weakness of God is incomparable strength. What is so solid that God's love cannot overcome it? My rocklike insensitivity can change to molten lava; my solid ice can melt into spring water.

Not by the armies of heaven does God conquer us, but by his sacred love—and my heart is captured.

That the members may have the same care for one another

(1 Corinthians 12:25)

Handsome limbs need no adornment, but weak ones require care. The suffering of one is felt by all alike. If my brother is despondent, can I be untroubled? The glory of one brings joy to all. When a sister is comforted, don't we all experience greater mercy?

In seeking the common ground, it is easy to overlook minor differences. But if we don't pay attention to these minor differences, our greater unity will be short-lived. If we concentrate our respect on a single member, it will be very difficult to put an end to divisions. Only when members have the same care for one another will there be harmony in love. To join the numerous members together, we must rely on God's love. If the stream of that love flows throughout the entire body, won't all its members be joined together?

This body cannot do without its weak members. May our hearts be as gentle as the Lord's heart in caring for them. The more solicitude we show over minor differences, the richer will be our common ground.

Sighs too deep for words *(Romans 8:26)*

I am weak. Overcoming the flesh is difficult. I resolve to do good; evil is there still. It is difficult to accomplish the desired good as I wish. The unwanted evil is done in spite of my wishes.

My desire is to show every care for the heart of the Holy Spirit. I want to be guided by the Spirit, yet I cannot help my sinfulness. I am enthralled in sin. It is difficult to keep God's precepts; I continue to act against God's heart.

My heart suffers deeply. The Spirit sighs with me, would help me—but I am ever busy about other things. My heart is capricious, restless, a jumbled thread.

I pray to God to help me that I may grow silent in God's presence, that my heart of iron may melt to flesh once more. May the sighs of the Holy Spirit, too deep for words, be my heart's cry, that in tranquillity I may receive the Spirit as gentle spring rain, silently falling, seeping into my heart.

Open your hearts *(2 Corinthians 7:2)*

The poet Li Si has said: "The mountain cherishes the soil which gives it height; the sea does not disdain the water which gives it depth." The boundaries of the realm of the Spirit depend on the narrowness or breadth of the heart.

If our embrace is narrow, we cannot put our arms about another. If we are partial to our own group or attack those who are different, this too is displeasing to God. If we take every small thing to heart, if we cannot forget past grudges, can our hearts be vast as the ocean?

The great land supports myriad creatures. There is nothing that does not feel the warmth of the sun. But how narrow my heart, smaller than the chicken's roost or the pig's enclosure; empty but for ambition. How can it soar with the eagle or race with swift horses?

I pray God to open my heart. Only then can I find peace. May it be high as a mountain peak, deep as the sea—when, Lord, when?

Out into the deep *(Luke 5:4-7)*

Simon and his companions toiled through the night without catching anything. But obeying Jesus' command to "put out into the deep," they caught many fish in their nets.

The prophet Ezekiel had a vision in which water issued from the temple toward the east. At first, it was only ankle-deep, then knee-deep, then up to the waist. Finally it became a river. Only when he ventured out into the deep could he see that the banks of that river were lined with trees whose leaves would never wither and whose fruit would never fail.

In the course of our spiritual journey, as children of God, we cannot always stay in the shallows. We must go ever deeper. In seeking the source of life, we must come to God's temple. But to find the fullness of life, we must leave the temple behind. The further we go, the deeper the river. Only "out into the deep" can we gather more fruit for God. Only "out into the deep" will we catch more fish.

Those who want to save their life will lose it, and those who lose their life for my sake will find it. *(Matthew 16:25, NRSV)*

If a grain of wheat wants to preserve itself, then it will always be a grain of wheat. But if it falls to the ground and dies, then it will put forth many shoots. If the five loaves and two fishes wanted to save themselves, they would have remained five loaves and two fishes forever. But given into Jesus' hands and broken, they were able to feed five thousand, with some left over.

To test whether one of God's children has life in all its fullness, we do not look at how much he or she has been given, but at how much he or she has given up. Spiritual gain is loss. The life of the spirit is death.

The way of the cross is not one of self-benefit but of losing the self. Jesus has become our water of life, because he gave himself up on the cross for all of us. Jesus calls: "If any want to become my followers, let them deny themselves and take up their cross and follow me. For those who want to save their life will lose it, and those who lose their life for my sake will find it." God, make us understand the truth of the cross and follow you along the path of self-sacrifice.

Again it is written *(Matthew 4:7)*

Satan's words of temptation to Jesus are by no means devoid of a biblical basis, and they are certainly not at odds with any particular biblical teaching. Satan confuses by quoting only a phrase or two of scriptural context. In so doing, he emphasizes only part of the truth.

It is precisely this superficial truth that is in error. It always is. Pushing any one facet of the truth to its limits in this way becomes a trap set by the evil one.

We must know not only that "it is written" but also that "again it is written."

God grant that we may store up in our hearts all the riches of the word of God, the whole word of God, and in its entirety seek the lamp to light our way.

And then come and offer your gift
(Matthew 5:24)

We are always concerned about the state of our relationship with God, but God is always concerned about our relationships with others.

God asks not simply, "Where are you?" but also "Where is your brother? Where is your sister?" Not every gift that is placed upon the altar finds favor with God. If something is wrong between my sister and me or if my brother has something against me, God will not accept my gift, no matter how good it may be. Thus I must first leave my gift at the altar, go and be reconciled with my brother or sister, and only then return and offer my gift.

What kind of relationships do we have with our family? with our neighbors? with the people we meet each day? Unless our relationships with all these people are set upon the proper course, our gift will always be left at the altar and will never be a pleasing sacrifice to God.

One sows and another reaps

(John 4:37)

The crops we harvest have often grown from seeds planted by others. Our achievements are built upon the sweat and strain of other people.

If others had not built the stairs, we would find it very difficult to scale the heights. If others had not paved the road through their successes and failures, it would be impossible for us to run the final length and emerge victorious.

Everything we enjoy has come about through the toil of others; it is always by virtue of the tears and misery of others that we gain happiness.

We take off our crowns before the eternal throne because only God deserves the glory. Each precious jewel on each crown is formed of the blood and sweat of others.

But God gave the growth

(1 Corinthians 3:6)

According to the words of a popular saying in the Chinese countryside: "In July, Mars is in the West. October is the time of harvest." Those who have watered the roots of rice seedlings know how difficult farming is. But we also know that the fields belong to God. It is God who has planted and weeded them. We have done nothing but help in this work, tilling and working together with God.

Though I have worked extremely hard, I have achieved nothing to boast about. I am certainly not God's only coworker. Some plant, others water, and there is rich growth. Everyone has sweated and slaved.

Though everyone has toiled hard, no one can boast of his or her labors. If the crops grow, it is all due to the Creator God. I can only plant and nurture; I have no way of knowing how seedlings will grow!

All growth has its time, as does the harvesting of the fruit of our labors. I do not pull up the plants to speed growth. I must wait quietly for the Lord's time. I know only that I must work and plough without ceasing, that I must be diligent and not idle. On that day when God comes like fire, it is God who will test the work I have done today!

My anxiety for all the churches

(2 Corinthians 11:28)

How heavy a burden can the heart bear? Yet the great heart of the Apostle Paul was ever anxious for far-flung places and the events of centuries past and to come.

Are not the weaknesses of my brothers and sisters my weaknesses? When my brother or sister is made to fall, do I not also become indignant? When others are anxious, must I not go to comfort them? Do not those with inner hurts that have not healed wait for me to come and apply a salve? Are the lambs hungry? Then I must feed them. Has a sheep lost its way? I must bring it home.

In God's house there are so many tasks that need doing. How then can I be permitted to sleep soundly? Thousands of tasks cry out to be done. How then can I simply take up space and eat my fill? The crops are many but the laborers few. Then the laborers must redouble their efforts. There are temporary shortages. Then the laborers must be all the more diligent.

Life is so brief, for we cannot bear a thousand years of the Lord's yoke. But though my heart is very small, it willingly beats in time with the heart of God. ·

Come away . . . to a lonely place, and rest a while (Mark 6:31)

Our Lord was so busy serving others for three years. He often went without sleep, without a place even to lay his head. He often went without food, enduring hunger and thirst without complaint. So it is not surprising that he needed a brief rest and went away to a lonely place. He did not do this in order to escape reality nor to get away from the people and lead a solitary life. He did it in order to speak quietly with his God.

We should learn from Jesus to selflessly serve others, to willingly bear heavy burdens, and not to avoid hard work. We should also learn from Jesus to frequently rest in the embrace of our God—to seek a place for quiet rest, in order to replenish our strength from its source. Action is like the pounding of great waves; rest is like the calm of a still pool. Action is like the rushing wind; rest is like the natural immobility of rock.

Our heavenly Father, source of love, is deep as the oceans. If I live in the sea of love, my love for others will not wither. God, our Mother, is love's source, hot as fire. If I live within the fire of love, my love for others will not grow cold. My love is so limited, while God's love is infinite. Only if I dwell in the eternal love of God will my own love endure.

With the Holy Spirit and with fire
(Matthew 3:11)

Christ feeds and waters his church not with the Holy Spirit only; he also sends down fire to burn it. He sends not only grace and pity but a sword. Always Christ is the refining fire that seeks to purge the dross and bring out pure gold. Like bleach he removes the stains from the cloth, returning it to its original cleanliness. He winnows without rest, separating the chaff and gathering in the wheat. Christ never finishes pruning his trees, cutting off the barren branches so as to bring forth good fruit.

Lord, enable us to know not only your mercy, but your strict discipline; not only your pity and grace, but also your anger and power. May your church, through the baptism of the Holy Spirit and through fire, be made pure and without flaw! Amen.

Go into your room (Matthew 6:6)

In their spiritual lives, God's children must have the experience of going into their room, of shutting the door, and of opening their hearts solely to God. Prayers offered in public are acceptable to God; but even more, God asks us to "go into our rooms" and pray in private.

God despised the Pharisees who stood like hypocrites at the street corners saying long prayers for others to hear. We are called to open the depths of our hearts to God so that God may look upon us. God despised the Pharisees' self-righteousness and their rejection of others. Their prayers were only for their own ears. We are called to kneel before God alone, with our hearts raised in humble entreaty.

God requires neither the empty phrases the gentiles used in praying nor the wild clamor of the prophets of Baal. When we wait quietly upon our God, the Spirit will help us to pray with sighs too deep for words.

O God, you alone see into the recesses of our hearts. We ask you to draw us near, to temper us, to allow us to learn to approach you in our private moments when we are alone. Amen.

Take my yoke upon you *(Matthew 11:29)*

God has never permitted his children to avoid heavy burdens. The rest that God promises is certainly not one of full bellies and idleness.

The yoke Christ bore was so difficult and his burdens so heavy; yet he found the yoke easy and the burdens light because his heart was gentle and lowly. Christ was obedient before God unto death. Faced with our own load of work, we always feel that we have toiled so hard. We feel burdened because we lack the obedient, humble, and lowly heart of Jesus.

We should come into God's presence and learn from Jesus' example—not in order to put down our burdens, but to take them up anew as the yoke of God. We should not seek to lessen our work but pray that in the depths of our souls we may enjoy the rest that comes from humble, obedience. A heart that rests in the will of God is able to take up its burdens as Jesus did. This is what Christ meant when he said that his yoke is easy, his burden light.

I was not disobedient (Acts 26:19)

The great light still shines before me. The tender voice still calls as it did then. Love like a rope binds me at your altar. Whenever I stray, love pulls me back.

Over mountain ranges, Christ sought me. Following Christ now, what are gain or loss, life or death to me?

My white-haired predecessors led the way. We, the younger generation, follow—some way behind—the baton passed, in our hands now. Can we be lax? Or waiver?

So many lambs are waiting to be fed. Lost lambs are waiting to be found. As shepherds, how can we not be anxious, burning with impatience?

Called in a vision—before that, tired, unable to move. Now, even if I had to crawl on my knees I could not bear to abandon the Christ who has called me. Called in a vision—before that I had become old, little life left in me. But now, watch me pluck up my spirits and run!

Biblical References

Matthew

1:1/60
1:23/20
2:1/26
3:11/83
4:7/77
5:24/78
5:17/18
6:6/84
6:28/9
11:29/85
16:25/76
18:3/27
21:18/40
25:21/30
28:6/47

Mark

6:31/82
8:22-25/36
12:10/41
14:7/42

Luke

2:12/20
2:25/15
2:30/21
2:35/26
2:49/29
5:4-7/75
9:51-56/37
12:48/69
22:54/44

John

1:11/19
1:23/59
2:10/65
3:30/61
4:37/79
6:15/70
12:13/38
12:27/33
17:22/28
19:18/45
19:42/46

Acts

1:11/54
2:6/57
26:19/86

Romans
        8:26/73
        9:21/55
        12:11/67

1 Corinthians
        1:25/71
        3:6/80
        9:15/48
        12:25/72
        13:8/68

2 Corinthians
        4:10/49
        4:12/50
        4:16/52
        7:2/74
        11:28/81
        12:7/35

Ephesians
        2:10/62

Philippians
        2:7/17
        3:13/51
        4:12/34

1 Peter
        1:2/58
        2:9/63

Revelation
        3:18/66